FREEBLEEDING

Wendy Allen's work has appeared in *bath magg, The Rialto, Propel, Poetry Wales, Poetry Ireland Review,* and *The North.* Her debut pamphlet, **Plastic Tubed Little Bird,** was published by Broken Sleep Books.

Charley Barnes is an author and academic specialising in True Crime narratives. Her poetry has appeared in the likes of *Anthropocene, Atrium,* and *The Waxed Lemon.* Her most recent pamphlet, *Unfaithful,* was published by Salo Press in 2023. Charley's most recent novella, *Your Body is a House Stripped,* was published by Broken Sleep Books.

Also by Wendy Allen

Plastic Tubed Little Bird   (Broken Sleep Books, 2023)

The Tricolore Textbook   (Broken Sleep Books, 2021)

Also by Charley Barnes

Your Body is a House Stripped   (Broken Sleep Books, 2023)

Penance   (Bloodhound Books, 2023)*

Safe Word   (Bloodhound Books, 2022)*

The Break Up   (HQ Digital, 2022)*

The Things I Didn't Do   (Bloodhound Books, 2022)*

Sincerely, Yours   (Bloodhound Books, 2021)*

All I See Is You   (Bloodhound Books, 2021)*

The Cutter   (Bloodhound Books, 2021)*

The Watcher   (Bloodhound Books, 2020)*

Burn the Witch   (The Black Light Engine Room, 2020)

Go on a Road Trip   (Wild Pressed Books, 2020)

Death Is A Terrible House Guest   (The Black Light Engine Room, 2019)

Body Talk   (Picaroon Poetry, 2019)

The Copycat   (Bloodhound Books, 2019)*

Intention   (Bloodhound Books, 2019)*

A Z-hearted Guide to Heartache   (V. Press, 2018)

The Women You Were Warned About   (Black Pear Press, 2017)

freebleeding

Wendy Allen
&
Charley Barnes

Broken Sleep Books

ISBN: 978-1-915760-97-5

The author has asserted their right to be identified as the author of this Work in accordance with the Copyright, Designs and Patents Act 1988

Cover designed by Emma Kennedy

Edited and Typeset by Aaron Kent

Broken Sleep Books Ltd
Rhydwen
Talgarreg
Ceredigion
SA44 4HB

Broken Sleep Books Ltd
Fair View
St Georges Road
Cornwall
PL26 7YH

Contents

Just before I bleed, I tell you to get on your hands and knees and bend me over, lift my dress and part my thighs the width of shoulders. I want you cervix deep. The next day run me a bath and watch the heat of blood make the water blush. Your fingers pornographic fast in this bloodied water. Hours later when I smell the cup full of my own blood, I ask you to go down on me and kiss me afterwards so I can taste myself. I know that you like this.

Dear Charley,

Today I was thinking about my visit to Wakefield in September. My period came early, and I bled into a perfect circle in the washrooms of the gallery leaving a paint-like trace I think Barbara Hepworth would appreciate, entitled *Liquid Form in Toilet Bowl*. I wonder what my body would look like if it were displayed on a plinth - *Spring* – day one of cycle, bronze with strings. I imagine the hole in the centre is the unspoken, the cervix when menstruating, the white space of unmentioned monthly absence. This smooth marble sculpture I construct all by myself, a tremble breath on each exhale, a blood-tinged transition from cervical ridge to the red pool of my emptied cup, the disc of blood too beautiful to flush. Sometimes I look into the sapphire of the ring I have worn for fifteen years, and the blue appears less believable than the content of my menstrual cup. I like how it stains the porcelain; I like the reality of art like this.

Wendy x

When I met my lover at the National Trust house (I will not give the precise location) my menstrual cup was as white as fairy snow when I pulled it out, as if lubricated by my lover's tongue. I am encircled by the thought that this is the reversal of too many made up stories, a bleeding finger replaced by my beautiful, bloodied vagina.

An aerial view of tributaries that maps the source for the deep end the dive into swimming pool wearing weights around ankles mimics the feeling of drowning. If you press on my stomach, touch on each individual tributary to see which date was missed.

I can't sleep for thinking about
falling – no, maybe diving, the clots
in my menstrual cup dropping at a
different rate than the descending
chromatic scale of my blood.
Unmentioned - menses - red exact
date. Today I bleed onto my skirt,
nobody can tell. I wish I had worn
white.

absence when do you not call / that wait / the paper remains white / cramps feel rumour heavy / you deliberately looking at me ~~you are not there~~ / caress the bed / roll onto the vulva warm space / feel the shape of your swell ~~you are not there~~ / bear down / fuck me from behind / squat over bath / work schedule interrupted by internal calendar / my feelings transparent as marble skin ~~you are not there~~ / the feeling of narrow when you are unwell / swimming pool / deep end

the canvas is white, framed white
| you tell me you love its cleanness
| the calm of the space it makes in
our living | room in which I bleed
so often but speak so little | of the
spilling leave blank spaces in
conversation | allude only when
I tell you not to touch | the frame
of me for fear of pulling | back
bloodied digits enough to make
you wince | the sight of my claret
not quite art to you | until I make it
so | its displayed on the towel white
walls where we entertain | guests
and I sneak one evening | while I
am pouring myself out | of myself
and I leave a damned spot | small
fingerprint in the bottom right |
and your friends will comment on
this | disruption in an otherwise
calm and you will know | what I
have done and you will tell them
this quiet violence | is what you
liked about the work too

lover tastes wrong on a tongue |
though you were the first | to see
me wet widened and o p e n | but
even now I recall the bloodied
palm | that had scooped me out
in hopes of finding feeling | and
instead pulled away flow | how
you panicked and rushed to clean
yourself | rid of me yet you hadn't
minded the last time | you fetched
blood

you use 'taboo' like 'excuse' | to
s e g r e g a t e s e p e r a t e p u n i s h
the bleeding | push womxn into
(m)otherhood providing you
don't see | life blood rush from us
| but can you imagine living and
never seeing | the ocean crush
the shoreline or the body | expel a
wave and welcome it | in that cycle
of things both o p e n and closed |
visualise this world wherein your
body works | to make something
raw and red important | only to
be fenced by parapets and tents
| that put a "safe" d i s t a n c e
between you | and the people who
expect you to someday bear | their
children carry their fruit in the
bowl of your belly |
split the peach of yourself | but to
not spill

there is a marble crack down the
middle | of the liner I have worn
for days | without incident and
with only a hint rumour | foetus
heavy in my belly that bloats but
never begins | to pass the promised
they said would come with
wellness | you   are not here and
I hum with the energy | of a womxn
waiting for the flood to find her |
at an inconvenient time | though
I would let you take me doubled
over | bent with a   cramp and
blood and anything | other than
your absence each cycle | more
than these   s of time where I
wipe and check | for tears of blood
any tears | in the lining formed but
you | are deep end lost and I am
kicking | carved empty and waiting

from this angle the bath reminds
me | of a conch shell opalescent
| with chemicals that are either
slick | oil based or sea water bitter
when I swallow | the bubbles are
leftover fuel from a bomb | or else
they are pearls scooped from the
innards of something | deep and
lingering in the basin | of the ocean
and when I press | my ear to the
outer rib of the roll | top it feels
like the earth tilts balanced | on a
trapped wave frothing at the edges
| grey all the way through to its
gut | reminding me I am made up
| of milk and elasticity these days |
white if someone were to scoop |
the innards there would be pearls
| or bubbles or oil slick and bitter |
but when I run my fingers through
the body | of water in front of me
still | I pull back a lost ruby a small
gem | turning it pink

you ask whether womxn know the
day | before it happens it being hell
| breaking loose from our bellies |
and I want to take you by the hand
| how a lover might and walk you
| through the undergrowth where
seeds plant | at the start of every
cycle and there | I will point and
here and there too | I gesture to a
network of nerve endings | and red
light signals that mean different to
stop | here they are signs of spasmic
movements | shudders so deep they
are penetrative | to the bedrock of
our guts | where you'll find layers
peeled and discarded | like old
clothes from a woman desperate |
to be touched coincidentally | this
too is *exactly* how I feel | the day
before this equator cracks

Dear Wendy,

Today I spoke to a man about
bleeding. He said, It sounds
complicated for women. Are
there signs? he asked then, Or
does all hell break loose one day?
It hadn't occurred to me those
who don't bleed mightn't know
the cat's cradle intricacy of life for
those who do. I felt I'd dropped
a pill period into the bowl of his
tongue, watched him smooth it
over his teeth and palate and come
out refreshed. Take this, this is
my body, I wanted to say. Though
in many ways it felt like I was
the one confessing, rather than
cleansing anything. I didn't want
to be cleansed, either, so much as
muddied; digits dipped so that I
might finger paint a tally of days to
show him where I am in this cycle.

   In an earlier note, you wrote
to me of measuring the blood by
the cup-full. I've lost track of my
cycle from sickness – something
else we've talked about, too – but
it struck me that I can measure my
cycle, now, by how long a bleed
lasts: number of days. Where it

falls on a colour chart – oatmeal to claret – is important, too. Though it isn't an exact science. But the body seldom never is.

Our conversations have encouraged me to think differently of menstruation – that, and much of the literature I've read around the topic, too. In earlier days, I would come to this from a vengeful place: resentful of the way in which my body felt to be breaking down inner walls and crumbling to a ruin, only to reform and reimagine on a cellular level in the month that followed. Now, though, I find I'm thankful for floods: relieved when I feel the swell of pain and disheartened when the bleed that should follow this, doesn't.

When the bleed arrives, I suspect you – after me – will be the second person to know. It will be a short message: a teardrop of blood. The long fought for period emoji. Though I may decide to send you a small teacup, instead.

Charley x

menstruation is like friendship; we
speak about the taboo of a new friend

I can't stop thinking about this idea of meeting for a coffee. We'll walk round a physical display of our conversation adorned on the wall of a white art space, in my mind I picture The Hayward Gallery rather than Somerset House, and we'll walk around, view the art depicted in your poem with the fingerprint of blood and the letters we sent, and we'll walk up to the photograph of my full menstrual cup, the stained *Stella McCartney* knickers in a cast iron frame.

our conversation is white page
drift from sickness to friendship to
absence which I feel all the time
from when I bleed to when I'm mid
cycle and masturbate twice and
even that is not enough I want to
know if I smell differently on day
twenty-five onwards I learn about
feminine endings my lover wants
me more now thick mouthed and
greedy deep in swollen ocean in
many oceans round breasts I think
of a life raft pull to detach you can't
go back conch shell ocean fake
sounds can you hear the screams
inside ovaries swelling my tears an
exact match to my lonely cervix

I'm day six today. My urine surprises me by revealing the full stop end of period in the toilet. I boil my menstrual cup in the pink enamel pan. I like this ritual. I want to wear dungarees, white unstained t shirt, Chanel *rouge allure* 176 indépendante, start again. If it were spring, I'd open the windows, hang washing out, buy tulips in twelves, always yellow. But it is Jan 6th and minus two outside.

There is no pause. We don't stop talking about all our feelings associated with menstruating. It is like we're ticking off a bloodied bucket list. I've written before in a poem about how I find the syncopation in *America* from West Side Story to be perfect. When we talk, do you think our bodies can sense the shared sense of community?

I hate unexpected bleeding; this is
why I don't think menstruation is
a cycle, more a manufactured lie.
That skating glide on paper when
I know from feel before I see the
Benefit lip tint stain, the colour too
vibrant to be a disappointment,
that the red discharge like silk
becomes see through pink when
submerged in dirty water, like when
my stomach plummets in a bath too
deep and my pubic hair is covered
by the shadow from the rim, and I
lie back, hair under rough tide, sea
grass busy.

when I tell him I am bleeding he looks at me like I am shit and I wish I could tell him I sit on the toilet and smell the insides of my menstrual cup and how I note how it varies from month to month, from sweet brioche to sickened heartache, that I know my own smell and as I dip in my little finger in I feel as warm as the inside of my cup like pink cheek, on post orgasm face and I feel closer to the blood inside than to him.

Dear Charley,

I feel like I am having tendon surgery without anaesthetic, that my insides are being pulled out with a knitting needle, tighter! pull harder! my womb pulled through my vagina, through my beautiful vulva and into a soft parachute, today landing silk blood O on crotch, with the aesthetic I feel when I climax and spill volcano onto seven-hundred and fifty thread count sheets. The irony – the reason we ruin beautiful fabrics flows from the most beautiful part of us. A cervix is far prettier than the Zara floral dress I wear repeatedly. I loved our talk about the Tracey Emin tent and how we could list all of the places we have bled. How about a David Attenborough documentary? Where my menstrual cup is observed through a blood splattered lens we watch as my cup swells, the silicon ripe full of clot muddled blood. The view from the lens an intermittent signal disrupted by red cramped wave. I want to see me orgasm internally. Does my red centre boil like lava like I feel it does, highlighting masturbation as a central motif in menstruation for me? I love the speed which my bloodied fingers rub and how my clitoris is as sensitive as I am when I bleed. We can watch birth, none of the 29.3ml spilt as the cup is removed. My years as cabin crew balancing first class Merlot on a tray during turbulence perfect practise, how this removal of full menstrual cup is the equivalent force of an aborted take-off, yet emerges perfectly, complete in upright stemmed glass. I think of my menstrual cup balanced between the walls of my cervix, held in place by science I don't really understand. I told you I spend hours looking at medical slides of the cervix, what I didn't tell you was that the sight of the bloodied tears emerging from anonymous cervixes makes me cry. This morning I spilt my menstrual cup deliberately, half dropped down thigh to the inside of knee, I needed to see this. We've spoken about free bleeding, you introduced me to this. I want us to do this through speech. I want to know that the little cups of loss I toss into the toilet or splatter across the bottom of the shower like a massacre, aren't hidden. Today I saw my bleeding as a sculpture, the blood the central theme, tiny tributaries in the creases of paper. I think these moments should be recorded. I don't really want to bleed in silence anymore, hide the fact I bleed as well as masturbate. To replicate the paint I make organically would be impossible. This should be celebrated. I bled onto my beautiful blue tiles today and I thought of how I wanted to show you.

Wendy x

I think of feminine endings | the
lonely fake sounds that stem | from
lovers not knowing the greed |
greedy deep ocean of my body and
the life | raft pull that comes after
the sickness | of the cycle but before
the shedding | and I detach from
them to masturbate | swell inside
and let tears come as I | the only
exact match go back | to my cunt as
a conch shell | salt deep and swollen
a brine tide | do I seem different now

Dear Wendy,

Today I was out with a friend.
When I poured berry and hibiscus
tea I thought of our talks. The
water was pale pink; the tea not
brewed. It swam with colour when
I next filled my cup, though, a
darker shade, cherry that bloomed
into something angry. Soon, clots
of berries tumbled from the spout.

I spoke to my friend, too, of
these deep and penetrative pains
in my pelvis. Sometimes, it's hard
to tell whether they're emanating
from stomach or sex.

The bleed is days late, still, with
nothing more than these pains to
show. It reminds me of your talk of
a lover; the vision of your period
as someone you are intimate with,
someone you are waiting for the
arrival of.

When I shift I feel the sensation
of losing blood. Each trip to the
bathroom fills me anticipation;
I expect to find my underwear
smudged with colour. Instead, I
only find milk-plasma; an absence.
It is a phantom, this month, I've
decided. I will shift and move

uncomfortably, expectant of stains on bright blue jeans or a tacky sensation in the gusset of 80 denier tights. The pains will only compound this; add to suspense of will-it-won't-it arrive. I imagine myself trying, though, my innards squeezing their elbows to their sides and pushing, pushing.

Charley x

are you okay | we don't have the
time to remove | jeans only push
them to hip level | I am so much
aqua water below | the waistline
it feels like I might flood | if you
don't touch me and if you do |
are you okay | and when fingers
test the reflex | how a back arches
at the contact | we both forget
how to breathe | though you
remember how to push | are you
okay | replacing the roots of a
plant | to the bed of the earth you
enter | slowly at first and feel | the
braille of my innards writing | all
so distinctly me that I keep it |
stashed behind my vulva and other
place names | are you okay | and
I feel this swelling from friction |
the slight press and circle clench
O | and I wish I could see | where
things have been readying | might
this bring the blush | are you okay
    are you okay
        are you bleeding

Dear Charley,

The other day you share with me how when you were in bed with your lover, you could feel the phantom bleed appear, your post sex discharge a warm raspberry ripple: white climax swirled with the imaginary, red heat of fresh menstrual blood. How much of our life is spent dreading the imaginary shadow's appearance, a circle the size of seen spread on blue based expensive woollen chair, snail shine rouged down line of back of *Sweaty Betty* leggings. your mouth, emerging red beet, a fantasy for me after A. recommends *Fear of Flying* and I turned down the corner of the page so I could masturbate over this in the bath.

Our cycles are not the same, mine shortening, yours recovering. You sent me a letter yesterday as if you knew I was ovulating and couldn't write a thing. And I knew then that we were already in synch.

Wendy x

Dear Wendy,

I am overdue poetry for you. But yesterday something happened that I felt moved to prose for: it came.

Without pain or forewarning, there was no knit-stitch-thread in my insides nor a pneumatic shudder. Gently, it arrived. You'll know, when the bleed comes it can sometimes come slowly with strings of mis-colour, but it moved through that without my knowing. Toilet paper became a ripening strawberry colour-change-quiet from textured white with seeds of pattern through to blush pink in a perfect two pound and I threw my head back to smile like a teenage version of myself might have done the day before taking a clear blue.

You were the first person I thought to tell. It has been so long since I found this tender joy in my body.

Charley x

My mother called it bloating. Is
that what this? A swell where my
innards become too big for my
body. I speak of it with inherited
language, resort to my mother's
tongue. Though she never taught
words like womb or vulva or
ovulation discharge, even though
I would spend so long needing
these things and the bloodied bits
between. Instead, only taught
"monthly", only taught "lady parts",
"bloating". Words that don't help
me to explain how my sex might
try to elbow free of my pelvis; a red
sea opening, metaphysical fullness
on day three of my mother's hand-
me-down bleed. Society rests on
silence and deafness. Advises that
we don't bloat with lexis we don't
need. But I want to speak it all,
now.

it ends too soon the full stop | that
might be a comma semi-colon |
though my sex can't be bound | by
secondary clauses or addendum
tissue wipes | tissue away the
last shades of the cycle | walnut
cinnamon tawny russet almond
| copper coloured urine | though
a three day bleed is better | than
continued   blank   spaces

the irony isn't lost; this pressure I,
too, place my body under

it's not what she needs, though
what she's used to

when we talk, do you think our bodies can sense the shared sense of community? I am sitting in a window seven days wide where I should be filling Bodyform but instead I feel a discordance. Through this window I see myself at a table; the wooden sort situated outside of public houses. The scenery is beautiful and the sky is blue but my body and I aren't on speaking terms.

I am becoming hypersensitive |
to red shades in my bookshelves
| blank early morning skies
before blue | taints the peach tip
beginnings | of a sanitary fresh day |
I find a yearning for a spin | cycle to
shake my sex | tissue loose from the
core | taint my underwear the red |
of *Deaf Republic* or *Bloody Amazing*
or the lettering | on the spine of
Come As You Are

i.   menstruation is a cycle

ii.   try not to exercise

iii.   try to exercise

iv.   don't shower

v.   don't have sex

vi.   don't touch your body

vii.   don't let anyone else
touch your body

viii.   sync with those closest

ix.   remember this is when
you're weak

x.   eat more

xi.   bloat

xii.   count the days ~~there will
always be 28 days~~

xiii.   this is when you're dirty

isn't abjection sexy he says | when
his insides are outside | of me
running down thighs puddling |
on bedsheets the colour of coal | a
small smudge of him crusted | on
linens that don't show | the spilling
of my innards dirtier | than his
somehow unwelcome | between
the walls of bedroom | where
he can leak limp to bathroom |
unashamed while I clutch hand to
sex | hope the most natural thing |
about me doesn't show | before I
shower back to being object

I kneel on my bathmat (the mustard one which looks like it is made from six thousand and seven follicles) legs as wide as apart as my last period, nipples showing. I insert two fingers slowly then pull out to rub over my now swollen clitoris. What do I think of at this point - the colour blue of desolate swimming pool a shallow wave in deep end how the electrical feeling from your thumb is fuchsia through my closed eyes it is 11.44 in the morning and how do I measure this point, the precise mathematics of degrees in which I fall

I try again. Hold on to the bath's edge (point A) and get ready to memorise this part where my lover is on a bed on top of the white *Habitat* duvet (point B) and the window is open and a spider plant sits on a reconditioned oak shelf and Beth Orton is on the record player and the window is open and my lover is pulling out my menstrual cup and it spills and he is fucking me in front of the open window and my careful calculations disappear, my working out crased by my lover's mouth. I was never good at maths.

I think of the mathematics in moments: the angles we bend to when thinking of one thing but simultaneously reflecting on another. If a climax leaves point A at this time but the worry about how my body looks during climax leaves point B at this time, what is the equation for their collision?

Though this isn't exclusive to pleasure.

Compliments, kind moments with family members, the word tree I might draft from finding an ex-partner's t-shirt at the back of a drawer. I'm there but not present. Kite in rough gales lost. Following the string might source some sort of grounding.

In the same way I might think of a bleed while with a lover. Rather than thinking of my lover, or how these moments with them are, or feel.

I'm always lost somewhere in the chambers of the wrong moment.

Acknowledgements

LAY OUT YOUR UNREST

Milton Keynes UK
Ingram Content Group UK Ltd.
UKHW020819300524
443394UK00003B/115

9 781915 760975